CREATIVE COLORING
Feel good

GALLERY BOOKS

New York   London   Toronto   Sydney   New Delhi

G

Gallery Books
An Imprint of Simon & Schuster, Inc.
1230 Avenue of the Americas
New York, NY 10020

First Gallery Books trade paperback edition January 2017

GALLERY BOOKS and colophon are registered trademarks of Simon & Schuster, Inc.

For information about special discounts for bulk purchases, please contact Simon &
Schuster Special Sales at 1-866-506-1949 or business@simonandschuster.com

The Simon & Schuster Speakers Bureau can bring authors to your live event.
For more information or to book an event contact the Simon & Schuster Speakers
Bureau at 1-866-248-3049 or visit our website at www.simonspeakers.com.

Manufactured in the United States of America

10 9 8 7 6 5 4 3 2

ISBN 978-1-5011-6232-9

INTRODUCTION

There's nothing like that "feel good moment," when life
just seems right and things are going well. In this beautiful
book you will find lots of slogans, phrases, and motivational
sayings that are surrounded by pretty patterns for you to
color in and think about. Select a pattern or a saying that
appeals to you, pick up your pencils or pens, and start
coloring. Whatever your mood or state of mind, you will find
that the relaxation brought on by this simple act will leave
you feeling restored, refreshed, inspired—feeling good!
For hours of coloring fun and relaxation, all you really need is
this book and a little time to sit down and indulge yourself.

From

....

To

....

From

....

To

....

From

_____

To

_____

From

....

To

....

From

....

To

....

From

To

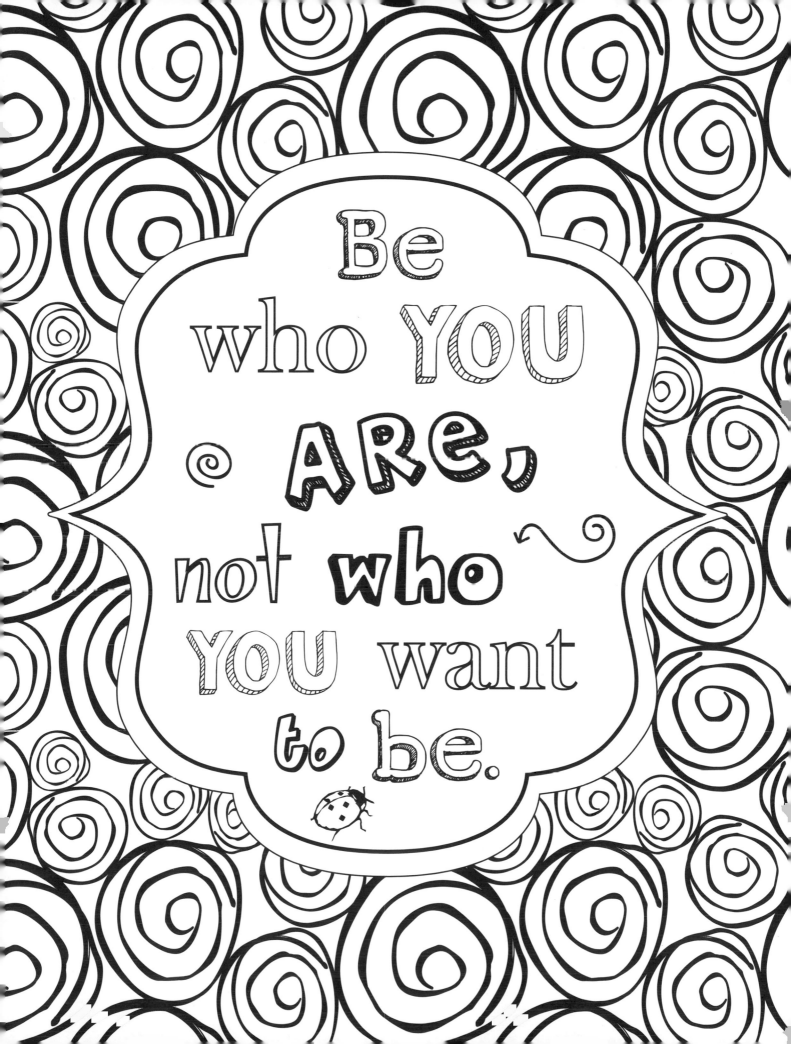

From

....

To

From

To

From

....

To

....

From

....

To

From

....

To

....

From

....

To

....

From

....

To

From

....

To

....

From

....

To

....

From

....

To

....

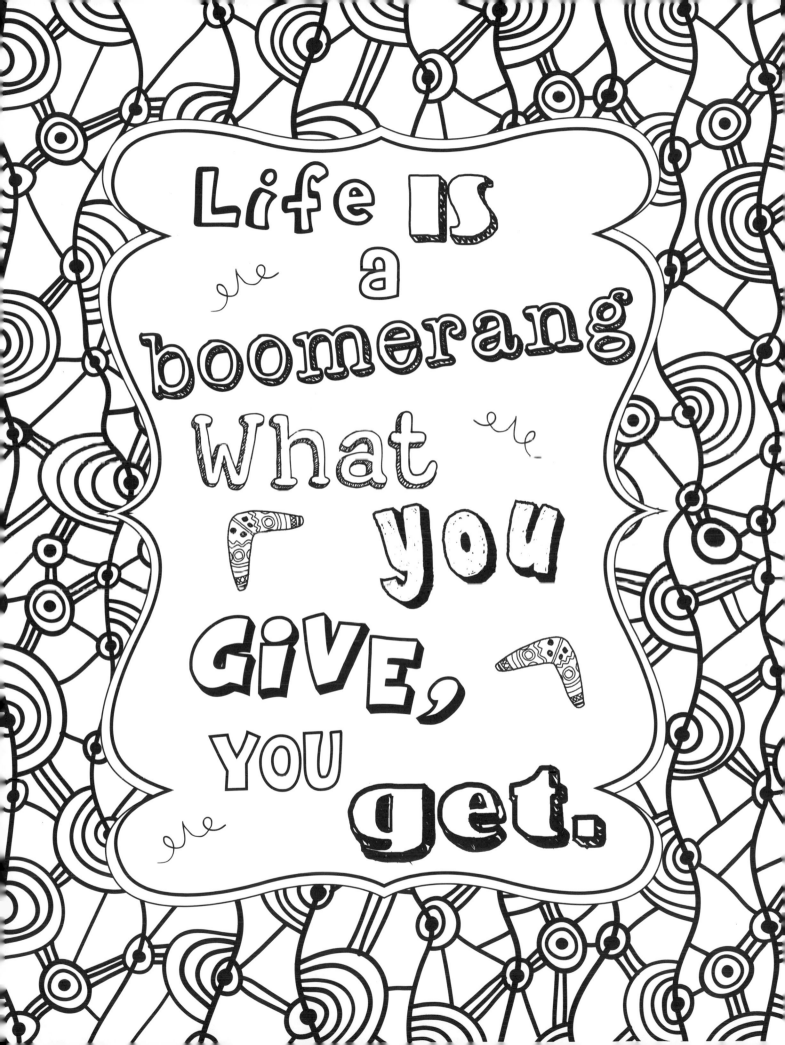

From

....

To

....

From

....

To

....

old WAYS won't OPEN doors

From

To

From

....

To

....

From

To

From

....

To

....

From

....

To

....

From

....

To

....

From

....

To

....

From

....

To

....

From

To

From

....

To

....

From

....

To

....

IT'S a GOOD DAY to have a good DAY

From

To

From

....

To

....

From

....

To

....

From

....

To

....

From

....

To

....

From

....

To

....

From

....

To

From

To

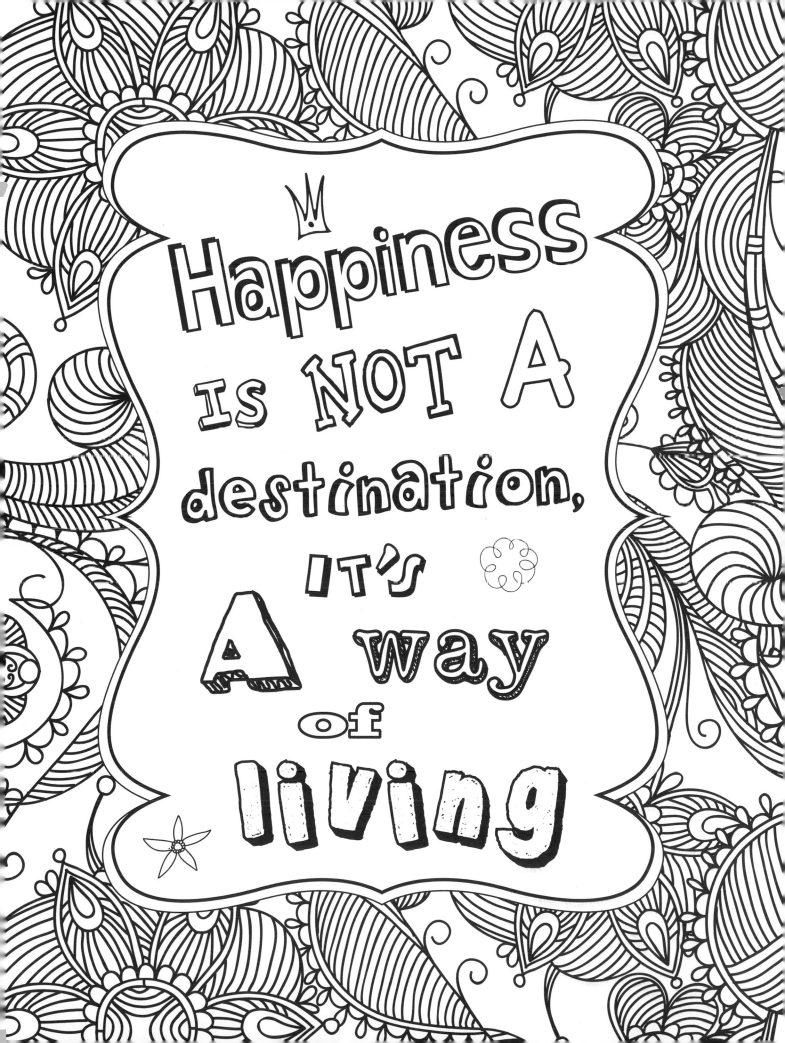

Happiness is NOT A destination, it's A way of living

From

To